Drew,

Congratulations for such a wonderful achievement! I know that whatever road you decide to take, your education and your faith will help make you a success.

Good luck in all you do!

Shaun

ISBN 1-58660-896-7

Published by Humble Creek, P.O. Box 719, Uhrichsville, Ohio 44683

Printed in China.
5 4 3 2 1

You Did It!

Ellyn Sanna

HUMBLECREEK
INSPIRATION FOR LIFE

$\mathcal{Y}ou$ may not feel you have much in common with the world's great heroes—but believe me, you do! When you take a look at their lives, you'll see you could not have achieved all that you have if you didn't possess their heroic qualities.

Be proud of all you've accomplished. Listen and hear God say:

"Well done, good and faithful servant!
You have been faithful with a few things;
I will put you in charge of many things."

MATTHEW 25:23

Table of Contents

Fresh Ideas

You would never have thought Albert Einstein would go on to change the way we look at reality. As a child, he was simply fascinated with light. When he should have been doing other things, he was thinking about how light behaved, wondering about its true nature. His parents must have gotten pretty frustrated with him. After all, staring at sunbeams accomplishes nothing.

But Einstein dared to look at the world in an entirely new way. He saw mysteries to be solved where other people simply saw an ordinary ray of light. And because he did, he accomplished something altogether new: He grew up to formulate amazing new ways of looking at time and space and yes, light. Despite his family's doubts, he did it!

The whole of science is nothing more than a refinement of everyday thinking.

ALBERT EINSTEIN

. . .

The mysterious. . .is the source of all true art and science.

ALBERT EINSTEIN

$\mathcal{T}here$ may have been times when your family wondered what you were going to accomplish. But success doesn't come in a single, one-size-fits-all shape. No, success is unique for each person.

Okay, so you may not be an Einstein—but I'm so proud of the success you've demonstrated in your life. You've looked at the world in new ways. You dared to think fresh new ideas. That's an achievement as great as any diploma or award you receive today.

You did it!

Overcoming Temperament

*A*my Carmichael is considered to be a great saint. And she was.

But she also had a terrible temper that she never learned to control. And she found saying she was sorry afterward to be nearly impossible. Doesn't sound very saintlike, does it?

But despite her fiery temperament, Amy Carmichael spent fifty-three years of her life taking care of orphans in India. She worked tirelessly to build God's kingdom by spreading the love of Christ to people who were desperately poor. Her angry nature made her describe herself once as being as ugly as a "slug on a cabbage leaf"—but she didn't let her limitations keep her from accomplishing great things for God.

She did it!

Walk with Him
as with a visible companion,
from dawn through all the hours
till you go to sleep at night.

AMY CARMICHAEL

. . .

Lord, do Thou turn me all into love.

AMY CARMICHAEL

You may not explode with anger like Amy Carmichael, but I'm sure you've struggled with some aspect of your temperament. All of us have flaws and foibles and besetting sins—but like Amy, you didn't let those get in your way. You ran the course put before you, and you reached your goal.

. . .

I have fought the good fight,
I have finished the race,
I have kept the faith.

2 TIMOTHY 4:7

He, who loved you unto death is speaking to you.
Listen, do not be deaf and blind to Him.
And as you keep quiet and listen,
you will know, deep down in your heart,
that you are loved. As the air is around you,
so is His love around about you.
Trust that love to guide your lives.
It will never, never fail.

AMY CARMICHAEL

More Than Ordinary

William Shakespeare didn't possess the sort of background that usually produces greatness. He was an ordinary sort of person from an ordinary sort of family. He simply did the best with what he'd been given, using every speck of talent he possessed.

And centuries later, his work is still considered to be the best writing ever created in the English language. He's been quoted more often, translated into other languages more frequently, and has inspired other authors more times than any other writer. His words have even become the metaphors and sayings we use in our everyday speech, and his influence continues to be felt around the world.

It all goes to show you—there's no such thing as ordinary!

Now, God be prais'd,
that to believing souls
gives light in darkness,
comfort in despair!

WILLIAM SHAKESPEARE, *King Henry the Sixth*

. . .

All the world's a stage,
And all the men and women merely players:
They have their exits and their entrances;
And one man in his time plays many parts.

WILLIAM SHAKESPEARE, *As You Like It*

You're not ordinary either.

You may think you are—but take a look at all you've accomplished so far. Look at all you've done and how far you've come.

Who knows where you'll go from here?

Wisely and slow;
they stumble that run fast.

WILLIAM SHAKESPEARE, *A Midsummer Night's Dream*

. . .

This above all: to thine own self be true,
And it must follow, as the night the day,
Thou canst not then be false to any man.

WILLIAM SHAKESPEARE, *Hamlet*

Facing Prejudice

Harriet Tubman was born into slavery in the nineteenth century. The white people who considered themselves her owners did not understand her value in the eyes of God; she was whipped even as a small child, and at the age of twelve she was seriously injured by a blow to the head from a white overseer.

But Harriet didn't let the prejudice of others keep her captive. After freeing herself from slavery, she returned to rescue other members of her family. In all, she brought approximately three hundred persons to freedom in the North. Despite the prejudice and cruelty she faced, her determination to help her people and her confidence in God never wavered.

'Twasn't me, 'twas the Lord.
I always told Him, "I trust You.
I don't know where to go or what to do,
but I expect You to lead me,"
and He always did.

HARRIET TUBMAN

In one way or another, we're different in some way from those around us—and human beings are often intolerant of differences. One of us may be shorter than the others. . .or taller; one may have a bigger nose. . .or a smaller nose; one may be too slow. . .another too fast. It doesn't really matter what the difference is; for some reason humans are uncomfortable with variety in any shape, size, or form. And as a result of our differences, we all encounter human cruelty in our lives.

I'm proud that you've risen above whatever prejudice you've faced. You didn't let it hold you back.

When I found I had crossed
that line [into freedom],
I looked at my hands to see
if I was the same person.
There was such a glory over everything.

<small>HARRIET TUBMAN</small>

. . .

I started with this idea in my head,
". . .I've got a right to. . .liberty."

<small>HARRIET TUBMAN</small>

Despite Mistakes

John Newton's life proves that God can use anyone, no matter how great his mistakes.

In the 1700s, Newton made his living by trading human lives. He shipped African men, women, and children from their homes to the slave-hungry markets in England and the New World. Many of the human beings he carried on his ship did not survive the voyage; those who did were destined for a life of captivity and hard labor.

But God used a storm at sea to change Newton's heart. Selfish fears may have motivated him to get right with his Creator—but Newton didn't leave it at that. He went on to change his entire way of living. Instead of getting rich from the slave trade, he became one of slavery's most outspoken opponents. Newton didn't allow his past mistakes to get in his way. Ultimately, his efforts helped bring an end to slavery in England.

Amazing grace! How sweet the sound,
That saved a wretch like me!
I once was lost but now am found,
Was blind but now I see.

JOHN NEWTON

We've all made mistakes. I'm sure you have, too. But you didn't let those mistakes slow you down. You stand here today, having accomplished so much, and all of us who know and love you are proud of all you've achieved.

Mistakes may lie in your past—but God's grace has helped you do amazing things!

Forgetting what is behind
and straining toward what is ahead,
I press on toward the goal
to win the prize for which
God has called me. . . .

PHILIPPIANS 3:13–14

Unlimited!

When Fanny Crosby was six weeks old, a doctor made a tragic mistake that left her permanently blind. Later that year, before her first birthday, her father died. As a result of these tragedies, Fanny grew up to be so neurotically timid that she never spoke out loud in public. As hampered as she was by shyness, emotional pain, and her physical disability, no one expected Fanny to achieve much of anything in life.

But with God's help, Fanny didn't let her disabilities limit her. By the time she died at the age of ninety-five, she had written more than nine thousand hymns, songs that are still sung today in churches around the world. Her disabilities didn't disappear overnight; she was blind her entire life. But Fanny learned to achieve great things despite her limitations.

Blessed assurance, Jesus is mine!
O what a foretaste of glory divine!
Heir of salvation, purchase of God,
Born of His Spirit, washed in His blood.

FANNY CROSBY

. . .

He put a new song in my mouth,
a hymn of praise to our God.

PSALM 40:3

You don't share the same disabilities as Fanny Crosby. . .but each of us has some limitation or another with which we struggle. Some limitations are very visible; anyone who knows us understands the ways we are challenged. Other disabilities may be invisible to those around us; only we know the way we secretly struggle to live our lives around our particular "thorn in the flesh."

Whatever limitations you've faced, you can be proud of the way you've overcome them. You wouldn't be where you are today if you had allowed yourself to be held captive by any disability, whether visible or private. Your achievement today shows how you have triumphed.

More like Jesus would I be, let my Savior dwell with me;
Fill my soul with peace and love—make me gentle as a dove;
More like Jesus, while I go, pilgrim in this world below;
Poor in spirit would I be; let my Savior dwell in me.

If He hears the raven's cry, if His ever watchful eye
Marks the sparrows when they fall, surely He will hear my call:
He will teach me how to live, all my sinful thoughts forgive;
Pure in heart I still would be—let my Savior dwell in me.

FANNY CROSBY

Conquering the Opinions of Others

Martin Luther King, Jr. was born into a world where African Americans were considered second-rate citizens. They were forced to sit in the backs of buses; they could not eat at the same restaurants as white people; and their children had to go to different schools. White people seemed to believe they could be somehow contaminated by associating too closely with their black brothers and sisters.

But Martin Luther King, Jr. had a dream. . .a dream that one day all Americans would be equal. His dream seemed to be impossible, but he did not let the opinions of others get in his way. He stood up for his beliefs—and because of his courage, he changed our world.

I have a dream that one day
on the red hills of Georgia, the sons of
former slaves and the sons of former
slaveowners will be able to sit down
together at the table of brotherhood. . . .
I have a dream that my four little
children will one day live in a nation
where they will not be judged
by the color of their skin,
but by the content of their character.

MARTIN LUTHER KING, JR.

You probably haven't encountered challenges as great as Martin Luther King, Jr. faced. But there will always be people who say, "You can't do it!"

"That's impossible!"

"It's never been done!"

"Accept reality. . .don't even try!"

Sometimes people tell us these things because they love us and they're afraid we'll be hurt if we try and fail. Sometimes our efforts may challenge others in ways they don't want to be challenged. And sometimes their own faith may simply be too small.

I'm glad you didn't listen to anyone who told you it couldn't be done. You went ahead—and you did it!

I refuse to accept the idea that the "isness" of man's present nature makes him morally incapable of reaching up for the "oughtness" that forever confronts him.

MARTIN LUTHER KING, JR.

When we let freedom ring,
when we let it ring from every village and every hamlet,
from every state and every city,
we will be able to speed up that day
when all of God's children. . .will be able to join hands and sing
in the words of the old Negro spiritual,
"Free at last! Free at last! Thank God Almighty,
we are free at last!"

MARTIN LUTHER KING, JR.

More Important Than Beauty or Prestige

In the Old Testament we read the story of Esther, a young Jewish woman who became a powerful woman in the ancient kingdom of Xerxes.

Esther could have spent her life being a beauty queen. King Xerxes had provided her with a twelve-month beauty regimen, and he lavished upon her every material gift she wanted. She could have been pampered and petted, spending her life in the lap of luxury, wanting nothing more.

But Esther was more than just a pretty face. And she refused to be cowed by her enemies. She and her cousin Mordecai cared more about others than they did about their own prestige or well-being. They spoke up bravely on behalf of their people—and because of their courage, the Jews won new freedom.

This girl, who was also known as Esther,
was lovely in form and features. . . .
And Esther won the favor
of everyone who saw her.

ESTHER 2: 7, 15

. . .

Mordecai. . .was. . .held in high esteem
by his many fellow Jews,
because he worked for the good of his people
and spoke up for the welfare of all the Jews.

ESTHER 10:3

You, too, should be proud of your moments of courage, the times when you dared to stand up for what you believed.

Passing grades, a diploma, and a promising future are wonderful achievements—but I think God is even more pleased by all the times you reached out to someone else, the moments when you put others' well-being above your own concern for popularity or material concerns.

Most of the time your small acts of courage and kindness will not be recorded by history, as they were for Esther. But that doesn't mean you haven't changed the world for the better. Even the smallest action performed with love has power beyond any you could ever guess.

$God.$. .will not forget your work and the love you have shown him
as you have helped his people and continue to help them.

HEBREWS 6:10

. . .

$Be\ strong\ and\ courageous.$. . $for\ the$
$LORD\ your\ God\ goes\ with\ you.$

DEUTERONOMY 31:6

. . .

$Each$ of you should look not only to your own interests,
but also to the interests of others.
Your attitude should be the same as that of Christ Jesus.

PHILIPPIANS 2:4–5

Freedom to Achieve

Watchman Nee grew up in China at the beginning of the twentieth century, a time when being a Christian was illegal in his country. Eventually, he ended up in prison for his faith. He spent twenty years there, and there he died.

But Watchman Nee knew that whatever the circumstances of his life, he was free to do great things for God. His books spread around the world, challenging Christians everywhere to live a deeper faith. He reached beyond his prison walls and built God's kingdom.

Nothing hurts so much as dissatisfaction with our circumstances. . . .
God knows what He is doing,
and there is nothing accidental in the life of the believer.
Nothing but good can come to those who are wholly His.

WATCHMAN NEE

. . .

Set me free from my prison,
that I may praise your name.

PSALM 142:7

Life holds many kinds of prisons. . .

* The prison of peer pressure.
* The prison of low self-esteem.
* The prison of past mistakes.
* The prison of our own natures.

No matter what prison tries to keep us captive, however, that needn't keep us from achieving great things.

I am so glad you didn't let anything keep you captive.

When you look back at how far you've come, I hope you feel proud. God has brought you a long way; you've worked hard, and you deserve to be honored today. After all. . .

YOU DID IT!

. . .

But don't stop there.
Be a true hero who changes the world.
Keep going. . .keep achieving. . .
keep making us proud!